WOMEN'S PROFESSIONAL BASKETBALL

Teamwork:

The

NEW YORK
LIBERTY

in Action

Thomas S. Owens
Diana Star Helmer

The Rosen Publishing Group's
PowerKids Press™
New York

To everyone who has waited or worked for a dream. Here's proof that dreams come true.

Published in 1999 by The Rosen Publishing Group, Inc.
29 East 21st Street, New York, NY 10010

Copyright © 1999 by The Rosen Publishing Group, Inc.

First Edition

Book Design: Michael de Guzman

Photo Credits: p. 4 © Bill Baptist/WNBA Enterprises, LLC; pp. 5, 8 © Ray Amati/WNBA Enterprises, LLC; p. 7 © Elise Amendola/AP Photo; p. 11 © Will Hart/WNBA Enterprises, LLC, (inset) © Nathaniel S. Butler/WNBA Enterprises, LLC; p. 12 © Andy Hayt/WNBA Enterprises, LLC; pp. 15, 16 © Nathaniel S. Butler/WNBA Enterprises, LLC; pp. 19, 20 © Barry Gossage/WNBA Enterprises, LLC.

Owens, Tom, 1960-
    Teamwork: the New York Liberty in action / by Thomas S. Owens and Diana Star Helmer.
        p.   cm. — (Women's professional basketball)
    Includes index.
    Summary: Profiles some of the key players on the New York Liberty professional women's basketball team and describes the team's first year in the WNBA.
    ISBN 0-8239-5239-8
    1. New York Liberty (Basketball team)—Juvenile literature. 2. Basketball for women—United States—Juvenile literature. [1. New York Liberty (Basketball team). 2. Women basketball players. 3. Basketball players.] I. Helmer, Diana Star, 1962-   . II. Title.
III. Series: Owens, Tom, 1960-   Women's professional basketball.
GV885.52.N4094 1998
796.323'64'097471—dc21
                                      98-16487
                                      CIP
                                      AC

Manufactured in the United States of America

Contents

1 The Best of the Best   5
2 Sisters of the NBA   6
3 Blaze of Glory   9
4 Heart of Gold   10
5 T Is for Teamwork   13
6 Serving Spoon   14
7 Double-dip Dreams   17
8 Off to the Play-offs   18
9 The Final Fight   21
10 A Whole New World   22
   Web Sites   22
   Glossary   23
   Index   24

The Best of the Best

The New York Liberty was behind the Houston Comets by thirteen points, and the Comets looked strong. New York was the best team in the Women's National Basketball Association (WNBA), and Houston was second best.

After **halftime** (HAF-tym), neither team could hold the lead for long. But the Liberty hadn't lost a game yet, and the team wasn't about to start losing now. The Liberty played hard and won, 65 to 58!

◄ The Liberty worked their hardest on the court to beat the Comets.

Sisters of the NBA

In the 1996 summer Olympics, the whole world watched as the U.S. Women's Basketball Team won the gold medal. After the Olympics, the team traveled around America and met their fans.

Fans wanted to see these new basketball stars play in their own **league** (LEEG) in the United States. So the men's basketball league, the National Basketball Association (NBA), started the WNBA. Women's teams would play in NBA team cities during the NBA's summer vacation.

Basketball fans in New York were excited when the WNBA decided to put one of its first teams in their city.

Many members of the 1996 gold-medal team, such as Rebecca Lobo, have gone on to play in the WNBA. ▶

Blaze of Glory

When Carol Blazejowski was younger, boys always picked her first for their basketball teams. In college, Carol was called "Blaze," and she set records for scoring. One year she scored 1,235 points!

But after college, Blaze found no **professional** (pruh-FEH-shuh-nul) women's teams in the United States. So she worked in the NBA's New York Knicks office. Blaze learned how a team works as a business.

When the WNBA started, Blaze became the Liberty's **general manager** (JEN-rul MA-nih-jer). "My life is basketball," Carol says. "Every day I think, 'This is my day to show what we can do.' "

◀ When Carol was in college, she once scored 52 points in a game at Madison Square Garden in New York City. No college player has ever scored more than that in one game at the Garden.

9

Heart of Gold

Athletes expect to win some games and lose some games. But in 1995, Rebecca Lobo's college team, the University of Connecticut Huskies, won every game! Rebecca was a star in college classes too. She worked hard and got good grades. In 1996, Rebecca shared Team USA's Olympic gold medal. She was the most famous player to join the Liberty. But she always puts teamwork first. Rebecca wants to help her team, no matter who scores.

Rebecca is unselfish off the court too. She visits sick children in hospitals. And she raises money so doctors can find new ways to help people.

Rebecca was one of three athletes to win the 1997 Most Caring ▶ Athlete Award for all the work she has done with sick children.

T Is for Teamwork

"If kids hear what I went through when I was a kid," says Teresa Weatherspoon, "they can see that all things are possible."

Teresa grew up poor in a big Texas family. But her family worked like a team. No wonder Teresa set college basketball records in **assists** (uh-SISTS)!

Teresa was tops in assists during the first WNBA season too. She was also named the **Defensive** (dih-FEN-siv) Player of the Year. "There's no question she's the heart and soul of our team," says general manager Carol Blazejowski.

Teresa Weatherspoon was on two Olympic teams and won a gold medal in 1988. Before the WNBA started, she played professional basketball in Europe for seven years.

Serving Spoon

Teresa Weatherspoon is called the Liberty's "T-Spoon." And Sophia Witherspoon is the "Serving Spoon."

Sophia played well in college. And she played well professionally in Europe. But Sophia wanted to do even better. "I need some good coaching," she told Liberty coach Nancy Darsh. Sophia wanted to learn where she played best. Coach Darsh saw that Sophia played best everywhere—in **offense** (OFF-ens) and **defense** (DEE-fens)! "I didn't expect to be a leader!" Sophia says.

Sophia dished up an **average** (AV-rij) of fourteen points in every game.

Teresa Weatherspoon and teammate Sophia Witherspoon are called "The Two Spoons" by Liberty fans. Some fans ▶ wave real spoons when they cheer!

Double-dip Dreams

Kym Hampton always dreamt of being a singer. But Kym was shy growing up. Basketball made her braver. After playing basketball in college, Kym played professionally in France, Spain, and Italy. She started singing at Italian clubs.

When Kym came home to the United States to play for the WNBA, she sang "The Star-Spangled Banner" at a Knicks **play-off** (PLAY-off) game. "Singing is still new to me," Kym says. "There's so much that I need to learn." But she's learned to let people know that she wants to sing. And she tries to learn as much as she can—about singing and basketball.

◀ Kym Hampton was Player of the Game in the play-offs. During her first year with the Liberty, she was the fifth best shooter in the WNBA.

Off to the Play-offs

After a successful season, the Liberty was in the semifinals! But the team wasn't happy. After making the play-offs, the team lost seven out of eight games. And the final play-off game was in Phoenix. New York had lost there twice.

Phoenix Mercury fans cheered hard for their team. Cheering helps teams play better. "We knew we had to work hard from the beginning," said Sophia Witherspoon.

The Liberty only let the Mercury score 41 points. No WNBA team had ever scored lower. The Liberty was going to the **championships** (CHAM-pee-un-ships)!

"Our team is united," Coach Nancy Darsh said after the Liberty won the first WNBA semifinals. ▶

The Final Fight

Now New York only had to beat the Houston Comets. They had done that three times before. But since then, Houston had won more games than any other WNBA team. New York was second in the league now.

Coach Darsh worried about loud Houston cheering. The Liberty learned hand **signals** (SIG-nulz) so Coach Darsh could "talk" to the team with her hands. The first half of the game was close. But New York lost the championship, 51 to 65.

"It was a painful loss," says Teresa Weatherspoon. "But I'm sure we will lift our heads and be back."

◀ Coach Darsh was proud of her players, even though they didn't win the championship.

A Whole New World

The Liberty's first year had been close. The next year would be different. There would be new teams to play in Washington, DC, and Detroit, Michigan. There would be more games during the season, the play-offs, and the championships. All the teams would have more chances to win. That winter, WNBA stars traveled together overseas, playing for fun. Coach Nancy Darsh, Rebecca Lobo, and Teresa Weatherspoon were the stars. They would have fun getting ready for another WNBA year. And next year would be different.

Web Sites:

You can learn more about women's professional basketball at these Web sites:

http://www.wnba.com

http://www.fullcourt.com

Glossary

assist (uh-SIST) Passing to a teammate so she can score.

average (AV-rij) The usual amount of something, such as the usual amount of points scored by a player in a basketball game.

championship (CHAM-pee-un-ship) The last game of the season that determines which team is the best.

defense (DEE-fens) When a team tries to stop the other team from scoring.

defensive (dih-FEN-siv) Playing in a position that tries to prevent the other team from scoring.

general manager (JEN-rul MA-nih-jer) The person in charge of choosing and paying coaches and players.

halftime (HAF-tym) When a game is half over and the players take a break.

league (LEEG) A group of teams who play against each other in the same sport.

offense (OFF-ens) When a team tries to score.

play-off (PLAY-off) Games played after the regular season ends to see who will play in the championship game.

professional (pruh-FEH-shuh-nul) An athlete who earns money for playing a sport.

signal (SIG-nul) A hand or face movement that gives a message.

Index

A
assists, 13
average, 14

B
Blazejowski, Carol
    "Blaze," 9, 13

C
championship, 18, 21,
    22

D
Darsh, Coach Nancy,
    14, 21, 22
defense, 14
defensive, 13

F
fans, 6, 18

G
general manager, 9, 13
gold medal, 6, 10

H
halftime, 5
Hampton, Kym, 17
Houston Comets 5, 21

L
league, 6, 21
Lobo, Rebecca, 10, 22

N
National Basketball
    Association (NBA),
    6, 9
New York Knicks, 9,
    17

O
offense, 14
Olympics, 6, 10

P
Phoenix Mercury, 18
play-offs, 17, 18, 22
professional, 9, 14, 17

S
semifinals, 18
signals, 21
Star Spangled Banner,
    The, 17

U
University of
    Connecticut
    Huskies, 10

W
Weatherspoon, Teresa
    ("T-Spoon"), 13,
    14, 21, 22
Witherspoon, Sophia
    ("Serving Spoon"),
    14, 18